FACING YOUR FEAR
OF TRYING NEW THINGS

BY MARI SCHUH

PEBBLE
a capstone imprint

Published by Pebble, an imprint of Capstone.
1710 Roe Crest Drive, North Mankato, Minnesota 56003
capstonepub.com

Library of Congress Cataloging-in-Publication Data is available on the Library of Congress website.
ISBN 9780756570897 (hardcover)
ISBN 9780756571559 (paperback)
ISBN 9780756570996 (ebook PDF)

Summary: Describes the fear of trying new things and simple ways to overcome this fear.

Editorial Credits
Editor: Erika L. Shores; Designer: Dina Her; Media Researcher: Jo Miller; Production Specialist: Tori Abraham

Image Credits
Capstone Studio: Karon Dubke, 20 (scissors); Getty Images: DAJ, 9, Image Source, 19, Maskot, 16, monkeybusinessimages, 15; Shutterstock: Africa Studio, 14, ChameleonsEye, 7, DisobeyArt, 11, Domira (background), cover and throughout, ESB Professional, Cover, fizkes, 13, Kapitosh (cloud), cover and throughout, Marish (brave girl), cover and throughout, Natee Photo, 21, Nuttapong, 20 (paper), Pressmaster, 5, PRPicturesProduction, 6, Sokolov Olleg, 17, vvoe, 20 (jar)

All internet sites appearing in back matter were available and accurate when this book was sent to press.

Printed and bound in China.   PO5130

TABLE OF CONTENTS

Words in **bold** are in the glossary.

TRYING NEW THINGS

Are you ever afraid to try new things? Maybe you are scared to take swimming lessons. Maybe you don't want to go to summer camp.

It is OK to feel **nervous** and scared. Many people feel the same way. You can learn to face your fears. Then you will be able to try new things.

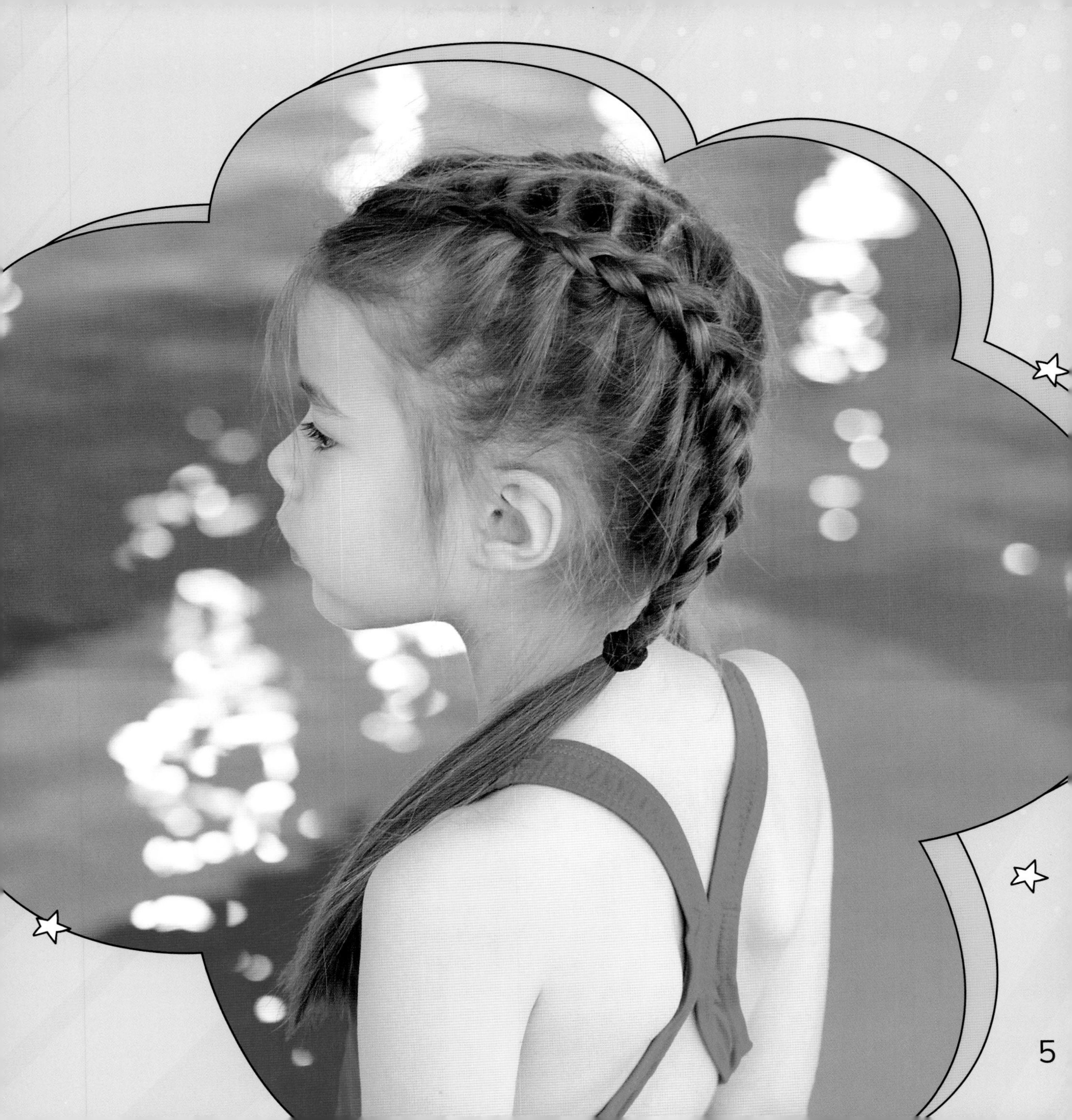

Why are people scared to try new things?
New things are different. That can be scary.
People worry they won't like the new thing.
They might be scared of making a mistake.
They can feel **embarrassed** and frustrated.

Fear is a normal **emotion**. It can keep us safe from danger. But sometimes fear keeps us from learning new things. We miss out on fun times.

PRACTICING

You might want to be good at a new thing right away. Does this keep you from trying new things? Remember to be **patient**. Learning takes time. It takes **practice**.

Think of a person who is the best at a sport. They are really good at it now. But at first, it was new to them too. They needed to learn. So they worked hard. They made mistakes and kept trying.

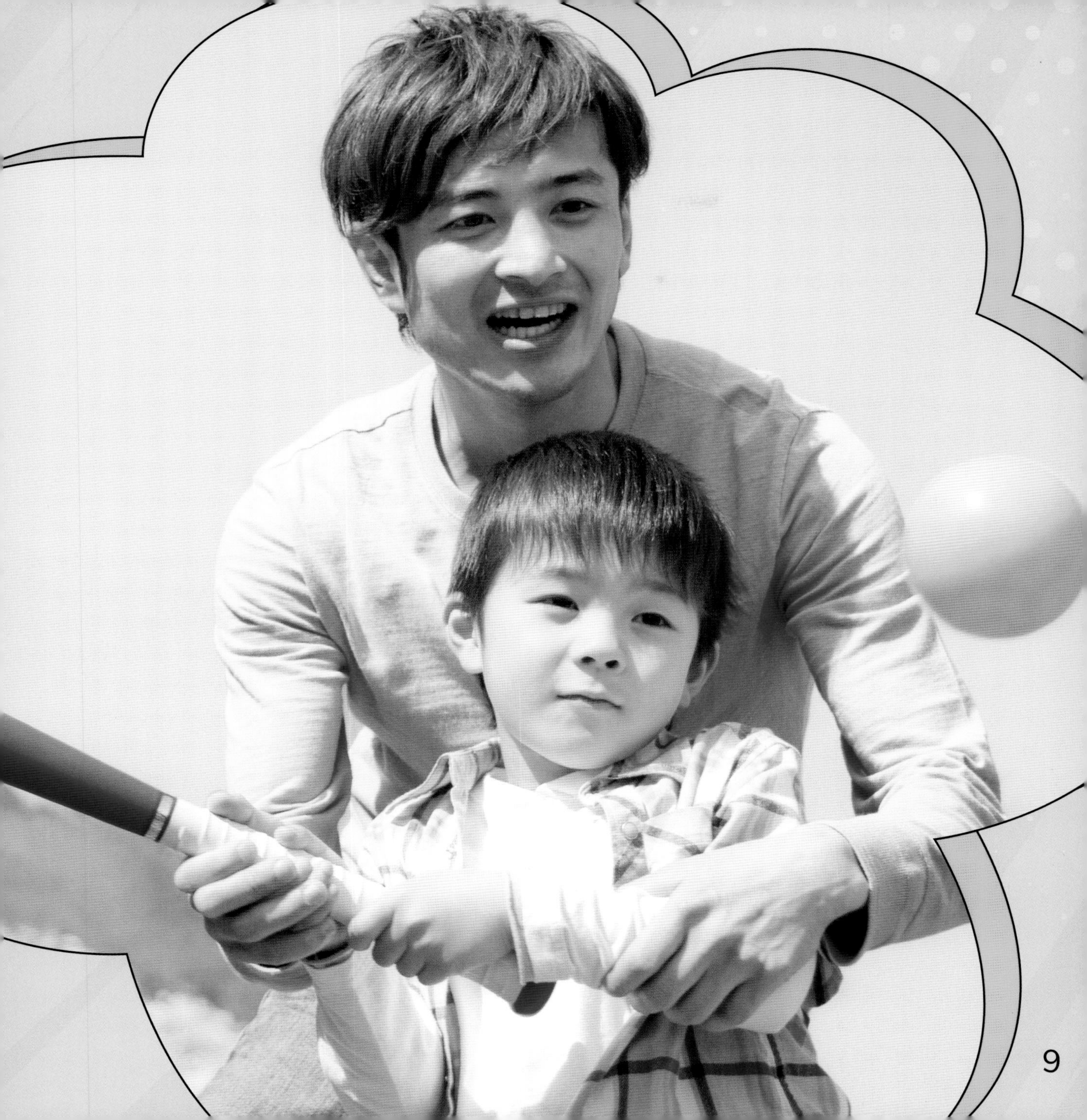

Think about your favorite thing to do. Do you like to paint? Maybe you like to ride bike. At first, it was new for you. Now you like it and have fun. So, you know that you can do new things. You have done it before. You can do it again! Be **confident**!

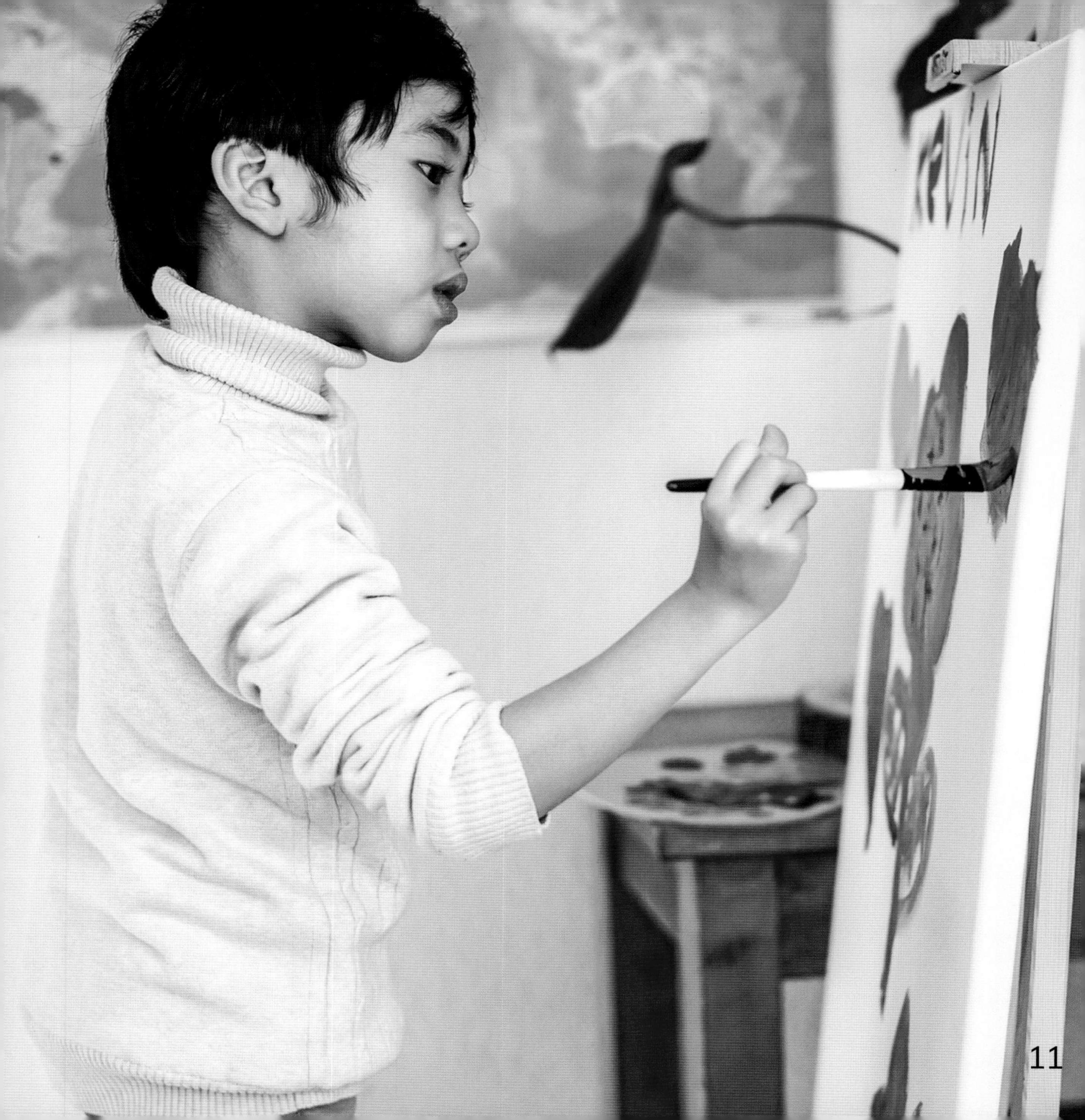

SETTING GOALS

Setting **goals** can help you face your fears. An adult can help. Make one main goal. Then make small goals. Make a plan to reach your goals. A **schedule** can help. Keep track of how you are doing. Did you reach a small goal? Time to celebrate!

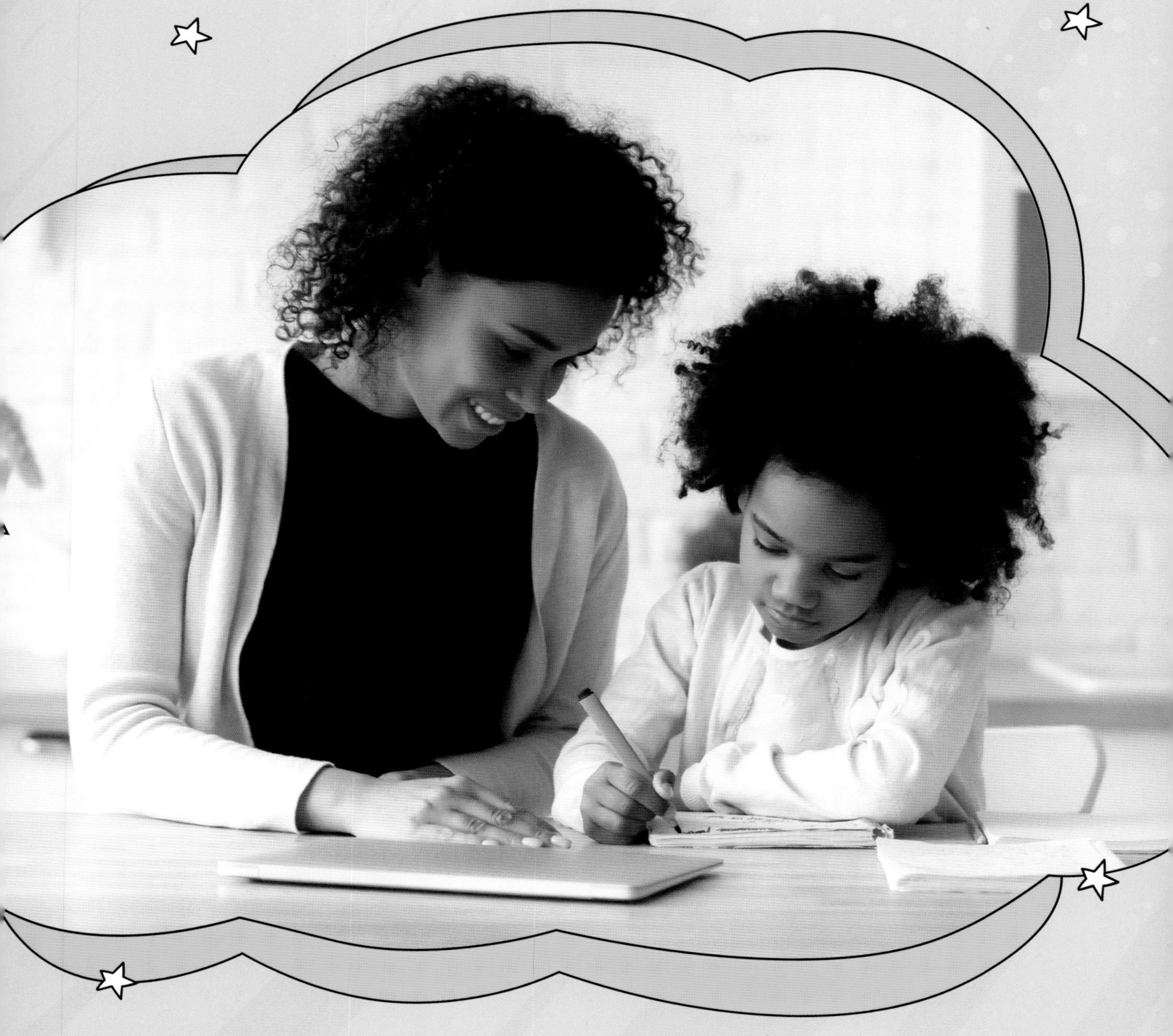

Kio is scared to talk in front of his class. He makes small goals. First, he talks in front of a mirror. Then he practices with his sister. Next, he talks with his family. Now he feels ready to talk to his class.

Nadia is afraid to join the soccer team. First, she plays soccer in her yard. Next, she practices with her mom. She learns how to kick. This helps her get ready to join the team.

When you try something new, you might want to give up. It is OK to feel that way. But it does not mean you have to quit. You have other choices. Take a break. Ask for help.

Watching closely is a way to learn too. It can help when you try something new. Alana wants to play the ukulele. She watches videos of other people playing. This helps her learn.

HAVING FUN

Trying new things can be hard.
Remember that you can do hard things!
You can do more than you think you can.
Be patient and practice. Think in a positive
way. You can face your fears. Soon, you
will have fun trying new things.

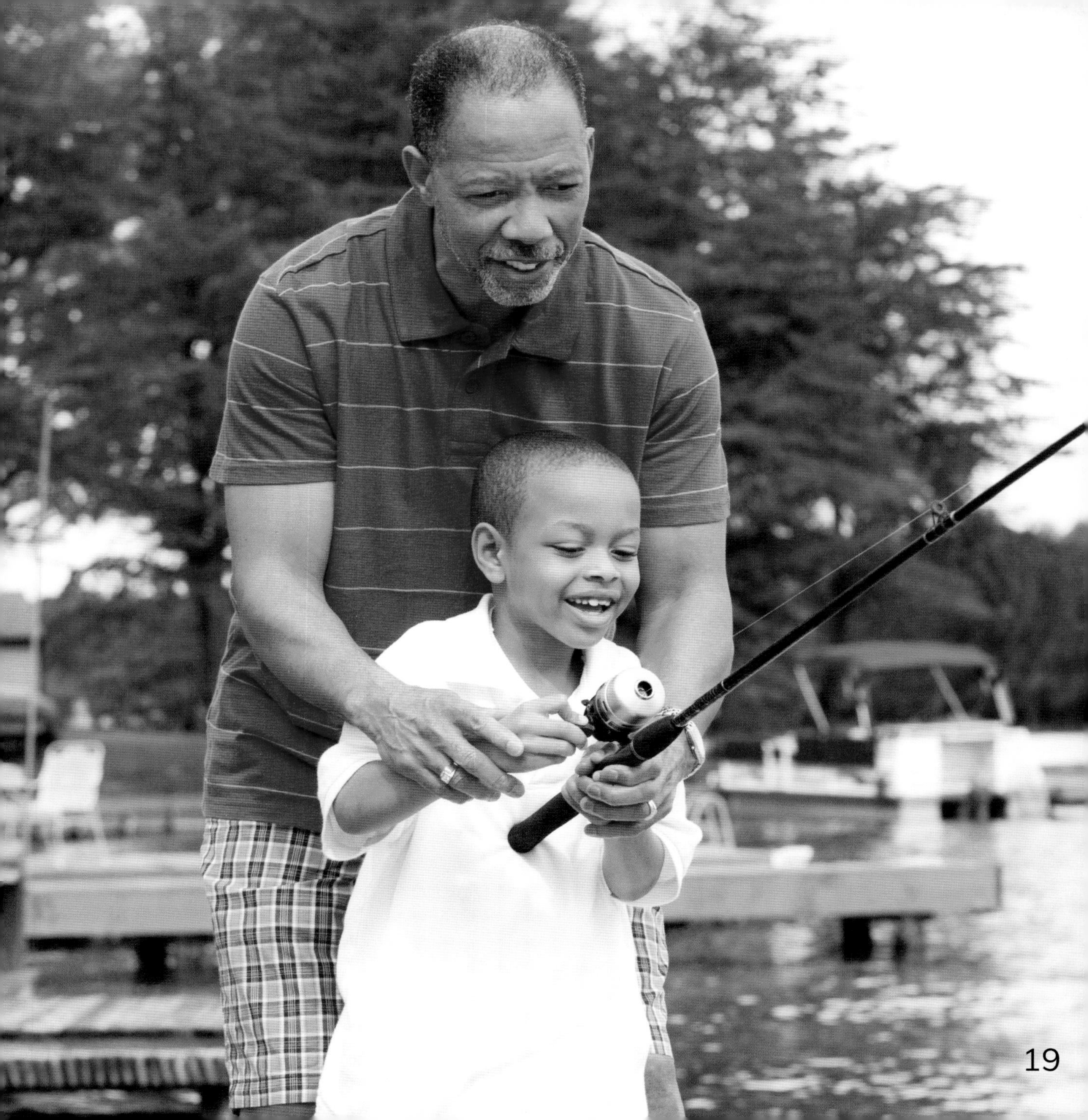

MAKE A "YES I CAN!" JAR

Make a jar filled with skills and activities you have tried. Add to the jar as you try new things. When you are scared of trying something new, read what is in the jar. Remember all the things you have tried. It will give you confidence to try new things.

What You Need

- scissors
- jar
- paper
- crayons or markers

What You Do

1. Use the scissors to cut several strips of paper.

2. On each strip of paper, write the words, *I can*

3. Think about different things you have tried. You can list new foods, sports, board games, crafts, and other activities.

4. On each strip of paper, write down one thing you have tried.

5. Put the strips of paper in the jar.

6. When you try something new, write about it and put it in the jar.

7. When you are scared of trying something new, read what is in the jar. This can give you confidence. It can make it easier to try new things.

GLOSSARY

confident (KON-fi-duhnt)—sure of yourself

embarrassed (em-BAR-uhssd)—to feel silly or foolish in front of others

emotion (i-MOH-shuhn)—a strong feeling; people have and show emotions such as happiness, sadness, fear, and anger

goal (GOHL)—something that you aim for or work toward

nervous (NUR-vuhss)—being worried or anxious

patient (PAY-shunt)—being calm during tough times

practice (PRAK-tiss)—to keep working to get better at a skill

schedule (SKEJ-ul)—a plan telling when things will happen

READ MORE

Harman, Alice. *Face Your Fears*. New York: Crabtree Publishing Company, 2021.

Huebner, Dawn. *Facing Mighty Fears About Trying New Things*. Philadelphia: Jessica Kingsley Publishers, 2022.

Mansfield, Nicole. *Sometimes I Feel Scared*. North Mankato, MN: Pebble, 2022.

INTERNET SITES

Fear Facts
kids.kiddle.co/Fear

KidsHealth: Confidence
kidshealth.org/en/teens/confidence.html

INDEX

ABOUT THE AUTHOR

Mari Schuh's love of reading began with cereal boxes at the kitchen table. Today she is the author of hundreds of nonfiction books for beginning readers. Mari lives in the Midwest with her husband and their sassy house rabbit. Learn more about her at marischuh.com.